You Can't Sell Stupid!

Chris Ashley

Side B Publishing

Copyright © 2025 by Chris Ashley

All rights reserved.

No portion of this book may be reproduced in any form without written permission from the publisher or author, except as permitted by U.S. copyright law.

Contents

1. Preface — 1
2. I am a beginner — 4
3. Sales Education — 16
4. Prospecting — 22
5. One Call That's All, Right? — 28
6. Sales Numbers — 30
7. Effective Communication — 33
8. Goals — 35
9. The Basics? — 41
10. Objections? — 44
11. Referrals? — 48
12. Paradigm — 50
13. Final Acknowledgements — 52
14. About the Author — 53

Chapter One

Preface

This book is dedicated to **Keavin Ashley**, my father, my mentor, and a salesman's salesman! He sold a lot of stuff over the years, but most importantly, he helped people with what he was selling. He made other people's lives better and never took advantage of anyone. He told me, "Do right by others and they will do right by you!"

This book is meant for you to read over and over again, which is why I kept it short, sweet, and to the point in each chapter. I didn't see a reason to write a long, drawn-out book that repeats itself numerous times like many other self-help books do.

I'm looking forward to you learning how to make more money! Some areas do repeat based on need, but they're not long and drawn out. You most likely don't need to read this book from front to back each time, but you may want to study individual chapters as you see fit. Use it to master the sales process, turn a weakness into a strength, and get back on track toward being the best you can be.

Yes, we can all fall off track from time to time—meaning we stop closing sales at the ratio we used to—especially if we don't evaluate ourselves continuously and correct our normal habits. My goal in writing this book is to help maximize your income. Over the years, as I've been writing and reading this book, I've used it as a guide to help myself. We all veer off track sometimes, and for me, reading the necessary chapters to get back into my sales groove works. I hope it does for you as well.

Ultimately, my goal is that you can go through this book numerous times, working through various chapters as you feel you need, in order to maximize your ability and profitability. After all, you're reading this book to gain sales knowledge and make more money, right?

I've been around sales my entire life and have had many mentors from several different industries. One of my all-time favorite sales professionals, who taught me a ton, is Matt

Dailey. He showed me how to help other people, instead of just looking at what I wanted or needed to make in terms of income. **In sales, helping others is one of the most important things you can do for people! If you're asking why this is, skip straight to the chapter on referrals and then come back to this section!**

I took helping others to heart, because helping others is what we definitely should be about in the sales world, no matter what sales career field we're in. Please take the time to read this paragraph over and over, because this is very important. We **ARE** here to help others, **NOT** force them into buying things they don't need or want! There will be plenty of salespeople who just want to make a quick buck. Do **NOT** be that person! Instead, help your customer see how your product or service helps and benefits them. **The people who help others end up making the most money in the long run anyway, so you decide!**

The title of this book means you cannot sell if you yourself are ignorant of the sales process and what you do—meaning what you sell.

I want to extend special thanks to Matt & Missy Dailey, who are special friends to my father and myself. Matt & Missy, my father absolutely loved you and your family! Anyone who has ever met or learned from them knows exactly how special they truly are.

I want to extend super special thanks to my Dad, who is now with the man upstairs! Thanks for grooming me all these years! I wouldn't be who I am without you.

I come from a family of sales professionals. What I mean is, I was performing mock proposals to sell stuff back when I was a kid playing sports—long before I was old enough to have a legitimate job, let alone know what sales was really about!

One example: I used to pitch my Dad, Keavin Ashley, on how I was going to sell chocolate candy bars door to door to raise funds for sports. He wouldn't let me go door to door unless he felt my presentation was ready. I sold a lot of candy bars, yet at the time I thought, "Why must I do this?" Yep, that was my intro to sales!

I must give thanks to another one of my mentors, Emery Shane! He owns a very successful commercial real estate business—might be retired by now—but he was one amazing salesperson and business owner. He told me that in order to be successful, I had to believe in myself, learn and hone my craft, evaluate my strengths and weaknesses, and build my weaknesses into strengths in order to achieve all that I knew I could. Emery, you have been and always will be one of my favorite bosses and mentors! He recruited me, mentored me, and then told me I must find what I love to do. Thanks, Emery! I appreciate you!

PREFACE

I owned my own company for over 13 years, and another company for over 2 years. I sold both of them a few years ago. I've been writing and reading my own book (this one) off and on this entire time. I own and have read numerous other books to help hone my skills—you should do the same. The time it's taken me to finish writing this book is mainly due to being busy growing my company, raising kids, and not having time to work on this book, sometimes for months or even years. I, like every sales professional out there, can veer off course, and when I sit down to either write in this book or just read certain chapters, it helps me get back on track to help my customers with what's important to them and close sales. Again, I hope it does the same for you!

Be advised: this book is **ONLY** to help you as a guide—a guide you can review time and time again while creating happy customers who are willing to refer you to others.

IMPORTANT NOTE: This book is designed to help train you to be the best with the basics, because being the best at the basics separates the mediocre from the best and increases your income. Think about sports! Professional athletes are absolutely proficient in the basics, and you should be as well when it comes to sales. Let's start from the beginning.

Chapter Two

I am a beginner

What should I learn first in sales?

Know this: Everyone, and yes, I mean everyone, has to start somewhere. Outside of my father teaching me how to pitch candy bar and lawn mowing sales when I was young, and after 8 years of military service, I interviewed over the phone for several sales jobs before finally landing one. I got the runaround like many of you. Heck, I was even turned down by my own father—not once, but several times. He told me, "Go get your own sales experience and we'll see!"

After being turned down many times, I started getting upset that I wasn't getting anywhere. No in-person interviews, no second interviews, no chance at what seemed like the "it" sales job. Out of frustration, I finally said the heck with it and called Terminix, a great company my brother-in-law sold for in Savannah, Georgia. He had connections because he was a "superstar" sales rep with them at the time. I had recently moved to Atlanta—yeah, still here! When I name-dropped my brother-in-law, who was at that time an Award of Excellence Sales Representative (superstar), I got an in-person interview for a sales position in Atlanta, selling pest and termite control services.

I had to perform a mock sales proposal during the process, but after all was said and done, I was hired! I was on the road to sales success—or so I thought.

What the heck did I know about sales? I had just gotten out of the military (no real sales there, according to civilian sales standards, or so I thought—yet all of us TACPs know we had to sell our Air Force selves and abilities to the Army constantly). My Dad, who had been in sales my entire life, had trained me for this day. Little did I know that all those mock presentations he made me do were actually training me. It was only when I picked up some sales books and started thinking "Oh yeah, no kidding, for real, I know this," that I realized my Dad was grooming me for one of the greatest career fields life has to offer!

Know this: Nothing in this world happens, economically speaking, until a sale is made. Sales is the largest career field in the world. Yet we have to train each other! (Finally, there are universities out there that have sales degrees, but in days past, there were only those of us who decided to write a book and help train other salespeople.)

Sales? Are you serious? Isn't this a field where anyone can join? No degree necessary? Why, of course. Some sales positions either require or recommend a degree, but in what field? How many colleges and universities offer sales degrees? Don't be discouraged if you're new—keep trying!

One thing that has continued to baffle me over my years in sales is this: Why does the world's largest career field have few to no actual college degrees? This was the case until a few years ago. Now, there are several institutions that offer bachelor's degrees in sales. It's ABOUT time! I mean, wouldn't an important job like helping produce a company's growth, in an economy as important as our global economy, have a standard of study such as sales? Doesn't a doctor have to do a significant amount of studying and perform a ton of hands-on experience before he or she can be given the title of Doctor? Answer: Yes. Back when I was in sales and a sales manager, there were no degrees, just self-help books. Which one moves our economy the furthest toward progress? Sales, of course! Hello, this **is** a sales guide! A tool to help!

Those of us who have served at a top-tier sales capacity must, at some point, teach. We need to pass down our knowledge, our learned skills, our practices, and successful habits to younger, more eager students of sales for our career field to survive. We need to learn about new sales environments that can prevent us from being successful, and those that help us trend upward. Many sales tactics of the past are no longer valuable today. Also, know this: sales is an ever-evolving world. If you want to succeed, then keep reading this book!

I wrote this book to be short and sweet with the intention of reviewing it over and over as needed to fine-tune your skill sets. Again, think about sports and how much time players spend honing their skill sets on basic fundamentals. That's what this book is for—to fine-tune the fundamentals of sales. In addition, sales techniques change with time, so I'm outlining numerous **basic** principles of sales that you need to maintain as a consistent process throughout time. Many of these processes will be adaptable as techniques change.

It's time to begin. Are you ready?

Many sales professionals get their start by chance. What I mean by that is some manager somewhere sees potential and decides to take a chance, or the applicant gets lucky that the company needs a warm body in a seat and decides to hire you. It's up to you to impress them—or so **THEY** think. Yes, I said that. Many (not all) sales managers aren't trained properly to train you (they themselves may be awesome at sales though), and if you want to be the best, it **IS** up to you to train yourself!

Alright, so now you newbies are in training (you veteran sales reps keep reading and pay attention too! You might just discover some new potential). As I stated, this book is about becoming the best on the basics, and in my experience, the people who are the best on the basics make the most money. Think about the Pareto Principle (80/20).

Depending on your industry and company, you'll have some form of a sales matrix to learn. A lot of companies call these "sales formulas." I've seen them go from 6-point sales formulas all the way to 16-point sales formulas. The point here is to learn whatever formula your company is trying to teach, even if you're a seasoned salesperson.

If you have sales experience and you've just taken a new job, then take your existing sales knowledge and lock it in a closet until you've learned everything the company that hired you wants you to learn. Learn it their way! Don't make that face at me—just do it. You'll thank me later!

Once you have all the new information down, then unlock your closet full of knowledge and integrate both sets of skills. Doing this will make you a stronger, better salesperson, and you'll make more money in a shorter period of time, making both you and your company happy!

If this is your first job in sales, here's your beginner sales model: Learn, Practice, Learn, Practice, Sell... Now, learn some more.

Once you have the very basics of sales down, fine-tune them. The difference between the top money makers and the bottom of the pile is that the best sales professionals are not only masters of the basics, but they've set goals, have the right attitude, and maintain confidence levels to go along with their sales skills. Plus, they utilize proper communication skills, which we'll discuss later.

The part I just wrote about attitude and confidence—you know this part—can make all the difference in the world between getting a sale and getting a no. Every single day somewhere in this world, someone can verify this with personal experience. I know I can tell you stories for days just about my own successes and failures, based solely on attitude and confidence. I've performed some of what I call my worst presentations ever, but when I had a great attitude and was confident that what the customer needed was my product or service, they bought from me. They knew I was being true to them and their needs and wants.

I've also put together some of the most brilliant presentations ever constructed, but either I was out of energy, my morale was low, or maybe I just wasn't completely confident, and as such, I displayed to my customer—in their mind—a lack of confidence in either me, my company, my product, or all of these combined. The result of this yielded me spending a lot of time performing a well-constructed presentation with no sale made. What happened is that I just went to work for free! No one wants to work for free, right?

Listen: Do you really want to make some money? If this is what you want to do, then check this out—don't learn from just one person, learn from many. Listen to what the top performers are saying every day. Speak to them and pick their brains, and if you happen to be one of the top performers, share your knowledge with others!

So, right now, what we're discussing are the basics. Most every great sales coach talks about being great on the basics. I'm going to tell you how to become **EXCELLENT** on the basics. If you do **NOT** apply what I'm writing, it's **YOUR** fault for not becoming an expert in sales and making more money! Do NOT blame me! You can study here, there, and everywhere, but do yourself a favor and make sure you apply your learned knowledge, or everything you're reading is fairly useless information and not worth the time it's going to take to finish this book!

So, you're still here. Okay, great! Now let's discuss the basics. Many people will tell you to learn the basics, but do they really delve into the murky depths of what the basics really are? We're about to start, but before we do, let me mention this: A good friend once told me your maximum money-making ability is based on your weakest ability. You need to look at yourself in the mirror, assess yourself realistically, and determine which skill set you need to fine-tune first (which should be your weakest). Be honest and realistic—if **NOT**, you're only hurting yourself! Work on only one attribute at a time, then re-evaluate and fine-tune again and again. I know that was way ahead of basic sales camp, but it's vitally important!

Here we go. Do you have your headlamp on? New batteries? This is going to take a little while!

When we look at the basic principles of sales, what really are the fundamental principles of making sales? Many people think that the basics rely on sales formulas or perhaps on presentations. Not so. Okay, so maybe it's the ability to talk to people and either get them to say YES right now or in the very near future, right? WHAT? What do you mean it has little to do with any of this? Sales are a lot more in-depth than just that! Let's take a look.

The basics of sales, most often, have to do with a very simple formula—a formula that can be adapted into any company's sales matrix. It doesn't matter whether the company has 5 or 25 different steps for their sales formula. What I'll lay out can cross-pollinate itself; you just need to learn it.

So, what are these basics?

Step 1: Learn your Industry (know your competition as well as you know your company).

Step 2: Who are my customers? (This is about figuring out your target customers. Who, potentially, makes up your best opportunity to generate and close new sales?)

Step 3: How can I find people I need to talk to (Prospecting)?

Step 4: Can you pitch? (Practice your presentation until you can say it in your sleep!)

Step 5: Can I close sales (Overcome objections and help people buy)?

Step 6: Will my follow-up be good enough to close the sales that don't buy on the first visit? (Some people require more time to make up their minds, and you need to keep in touch. Otherwise, the sale can go dead, and you end up with nothing. Also, some customers just want to see if you'll follow up before they give you the final yes.)

Step 7: Can I produce referrals? (Referrals are the most valuable lead you can get—forget gold, and treat these as platinum!)

Shall we begin with Step 1? Let's do this!

Step 1: Learn Your Industry

This means not only learning what your company produces, but what your competitors do and don't do. Take the time to learn the history of your industry. Where did it come from? How did it evolve to what it is now? You may not need to always discuss this with your customers, but occasionally you might. The importance of this is to help you become an expert in your industry.

From a sales standpoint, what you do here is ask the client how much they know about your company and industry, listen to their answer, and then follow up with how much they'd like to know. This helps open people up to having a conversation with you, as well as being able to tailor your presentation to them and their needs and wants. Remember, this is NOT about YOU—it's about YOUR customer! How nice would it be to close sales just because your competition didn't know or discuss this? It happens from time to time.

Does your competition do EXACTLY the same thing? Hmm. Maybe, maybe not. How do you and your company differ from your direct competition? Evaluate your company and learn everything you can about your competition. Figure out how you can stand out among the crowd. Standing out is one of the **MOST** important things you can do! Anyone can sell the same thing at the same price, or at a lower price. However, how do you differ, and how do you justify your price? **Remember this:** Price is a direct reflection of the value you've built as perceived by your customer. There will almost always be a cheaper price unless all you're selling is price and you happen to be the cheapest in town. If you're the cheapest, know this: someone else will eventually come behind you and cut your price! Sell value, NOT price!

Step 2: Who Are My Customers?

Well, just look around! Okay, so what if your customers aren't that obvious? Maybe finding out who you need to talk to takes more work than looking up from the book you're reading. Maybe you need to go to the tax office to determine who owns a certain property, if you're working in the real estate industry. Maybe you need to find out who owns a restaurant or other business, if you're doing marketing, pest control, soda machine sales, doormat sales, uniforms, etc. Perhaps ask those you work with or for about how you can find people to talk to and pitch.

Depending on the industry you choose, the customer base varies. If you can't figure it out, or you want a new base in the same industry, go ask the top money makers and survey potential candidates. Don't ask exactly who "their" clients are, but simply ask for suggestions on who you might want to talk to in order to grow your business. The crazy thing about sales is that the top dogs are just as likely to share their info, as they in turn seek to gain info from you so they too can grow. If someone chooses to exchange information and it's beneficial to you both, then exchange info back, should you feel comfortable. It could lead to bigger and better opportunities, or it could lead to nothing. There's only one way to find out. Do you want to get paid?

Step 3: Prospecting

Oh my! I hear that word every day; however, is it done faithfully or haphazardly? Yes, you know the difference between the two, but you must answer honestly. Do you just run the leads your company provides, or do you seek potential customers on top of getting company leads? The top money-making sales representatives prospect religiously! They don't sit around and just wait for someone to call in, which equates to company leads.

Prospecting is nothing more than going out and trying to find a new customer who didn't contact you directly. Think about this: If you owned your own company, how do you intend to get new customers without spending a lot of money on advertising? I can spend ALL DAY AND NIGHT talking about prospecting. The fact is, the more people you search for to talk to, the more opportunities you have to make new sales.

A good friend of mine (Matt, who I thanked in the title of this book) used to say, use the 3-foot rule. Meaning, anyone within 3 feet of you gets a business card and you introduce yourself and what you do. You don't have to pitch them right then and there, just advise them of who you are and what you do. Depending on what you sell, this could work very well. When it comes to prospecting, you need to determine for yourself what works best for you! What do you mean? Well, not all prospecting methods work for everyone, meaning what works for you might not work all that well for someone else, and vice versa. However, just because something may not work the first or tenth time doesn't mean you should abandon it. There could be potential. You have to determine whether it's beneficial and keep trying, or work on something else. Take in this information and evaluate for yourself what works for you and what doesn't. Your main goal here is to figure out what makes you the most money and work on those programs.

As far as prospecting goes, make a list of all the different ways you could find potential customers, then narrow it down by what has worked best, and prioritize it based on what you're good at. Don't ALLOW what you're good at to **just** be your only method of prospecting!

I've listed some prospecting opportunities that I think are pretty universal, but know this: there are tons of other ways to find business that aren't listed here. To find out more, do some internal research about your industry.

I. Referrals (Best form of new creative sales, period! Sometimes you may need to contact your current customers and ask for them.)

II. Door Knocking (either residential or business to business)

III. Cold Calls (Better get some really tough skin....)

IV. Ads (If your company doesn't pay for all of them, you may want to run some inexpensive advertising on your own. Might be a good idea to get company approval before running any ads though.)

V. Flyers (You can put up flyers in areas you know clients in your industry are looking—remember, company approval.)

VI. Canvas **YOUR** territory, meaning work your territory so everyone knows your name. Be the EXPERT! Do **NOT** allow your competition to know more about your area than you! Make sure businesses and/or residential customers know who you are, what you do, and how you can help them. Remember the 3-foot rule here!

VII. Network. Connect with other job fields from different industries that have similar customers as you, and trade info.

VIII. Many other methods exist, such as buying calling lists, door hangers, etc. Find ways that might connect you to a customer in need of what you have to offer.

There are numerous ways to try and find business as a salesperson. What you need to do is figure out what works best for you. Work those methods that make you the most money, then incorporate new ways to make even more money. If the methods work, keep doing them; if not, discard them. Remember this: not everything will work for everyone!

Step 4: Presentation Skills

Do you have the words that make you look like Rico Suave to your customers? How are your presentation skills? Are you at the top of the class in your office, or can you speak anytime, anywhere, about how your industry can help someone?

Presentations take a **TON** of work! Even if you're a seasoned vet, you need to constantly practice your presentation. Why? Does anyone in professional sports JUST show up for the big game? Doubt it! Most pros spend more time on the practice field than in the regular game. Why should this be any different for you? We do from time to time veer off course and need to get back on track. Think about the times when you were closing just about everyone you spoke with, and then you stopped, yet in your mind you're still doing everything the same way. You went into a slump. That slump is usually a direct result of veering off course! Slumps are normal, which is why we **must** train again and again on the basics so we can reduce slumps and yield the best results possible.

Knowing your presentation backwards and forwards can make or break a sale. If you're the best of the best at HOW you speak about and feel about your company and product, then you'll usually yield the most sales. Your customers will see and feel it too. Remember this: attitude and confidence play a major part in your presentations.

Step 5: Closing Sales

Uh oh... Time to ask for the sale (Closing). Wow, what an awkward time, right? Not necessarily. If you've done your job correctly—meaning following the simple steps above—the closing of a sale is usually the easiest part of the whole deal. All you have to do is figure out a way to get someone to say the FINAL yes, right?

There are TONS of ways to get a prospect to say yes. These techniques vary by industry, as well as the prospective customer. The most important thing to know here is this: "Does my product or service help my customer, and does my customer want and/or need my product or service?"

If the answer to this is YES, then ask for commitment. Remember this: if you do NOT ask for the sale, the answer is most likely NO! **You have to ask for business!** Many times, sales representatives do a good job presenting what they have to offer yet fail to ask for a commitment or ask for the sale. (My personal opinion on this is that salespeople feel as though they did a great job presenting, and their customer should just say yes, or an objection or stall comes up, and they're not sure how to overcome that objection or stall.)

The internet allows your prospective customers to be extremely knowledgeable these days, meaning they either know about you and your product/service/competitors, or think they know about you and your industry. You have to make sure you take great care of your customers. However, many of your customers expect you to still ask for a final commitment, especially if they themselves are in the sales industry. **Don't try to take advantage of your customers! Seek to help them! However, make sure you ask for the sale!** Remember, you want referrals, and you most likely won't get those without helping your current customers based on what they need and want.

When asking for the sale, what's the worst thing that can happen? Your customer says NO? Okay, guess what—the answer was most likely NO if you hadn't asked, so by asking for a commitment, at least you increased your chances to 50/50! **You have nothing to lose, so just ask!** When asking for the sale, remember: objections happen from time to time. See the following.

Here Come the Objections

When you ask for the sale, sometimes people give objections, even to buying right on the spot. It may take more than one meeting or conversation to close the sale. Hey, this is OKAY! Not all sales are made at the first meeting or interaction. Also, some sales that are made at the first meeting or interaction are not always made without overcoming some kind of objection(s). **DO NOT BE AFRAID OF OBJECTIONS!** Understand that most objections are nothing more than your customer seeking more information about what you do, what your industry does, who you really are, and/or a combination of these. Many, many salespeople shy away from trying to close a sale when objections are raised.

Embrace objections!

When objections arise, answer them, and then close again. As you become better and better at sales within your industry, do yourself a favor: learn, handle, and remove the most common objections you normally hear in your presentations before they ever become an actual objection. What I mean is, build into your presentation how you overcome the most common objections before the customer ever brings them up. This will make you better and make you more money!

Listen Up: Objections tell you either you haven't covered everything just yet, or perhaps your customer really does need to discuss with someone else before a final decision is made. However, a lot of times your customer will stall you with what seems like an objection only to put you off to another time. This way, they don't have to make a final decision right then and there. **Stalls vs. Objections** are extremely important to determine as they often can be the difference between a YES and a NO! Most often you'll encounter stalls, and you need to know how to overcome these before they arise. Yet objections do arise as well and must be handled properly, respectfully, and professionally. Objections are a customer's way of saying, "Hey, could you tell me more?" However, like I said above, sometimes we get "stalls," which are often confused with objections.

The difference between a stall and objection: A "stall" is nothing more than a customer trying to put you off, even when they know what you have to offer meets their needs and wants. They stall you so they do **NOT** have to make a final decision on purchasing your service right then and there. A stall usually leads to no sale, even in the future. What I mean is your customer agrees with you and what you have to offer yet finds a way to avoid making that final decision. One of the major reasons for stalls is that people don't want to be sold. Their most convenient method to avoid saying yes is, "Let me talk to my husband/wife/business partner." **Conquer the stalls by asking open-ended**

questions! Open-ended questions are questions that make your customers say more than just yes or no. Open-ended questions get them talking and telling you their story, needs, and wants again, so you can find a way to help and get back to making a sale. Understand this: you're not trying to take advantage of anyone by asking questions—you're simply trying to understand where the customer's mindset is at. Never try to take advantage of anyone, period! It's rude and disgusting! Be careful though, as stated above: many times the "I have to discuss with my wife/husband/business partner" objection or stall is very much a stall tactic, **yet could be for real**. You have to read the non-verbals and feel it out.

Most often, a stall technique is also one of the most difficult for sales professionals to overcome. You have to engage in conversation with your customer to discover the truth versus wondering if you'll make this sale. It's almost like taking a "who cares" attitude in order to have a real chance at winning. What I mean by this is, you ask your customer for that final commitment anyway, or you ask more probing questions to put them on the spot to tell you the real reason they're not buying from you just yet, and then ask for that commitment. Some people love to blame their spouse for not being able to make that final commitment. Look at their surroundings—most wives make the majority of decisions as it pertains to the house, so do NOT discredit the wife or spouse if you're doing any type of house renovation sales. Main point: treat everyone as if they make the final decisions!

If you determine that your customer really needs to discuss further with another person, then set a date and time to follow up. The relationship you've built with your customer will help you determine if it's a stall, or if they really do need to discuss it with another person. Occasionally, it could be that they actually need to consult with another person. Figure it out through open-ended questions.

Be forewarned: **DO NOT CREATE** unnecessary objections. Quite often, salespeople will create objections that otherwise would NOT have been there. In doing such, this can either stall the sale temporarily or kill it completely. **Pay attention**, because a lot of these stalls or objections are fabricated from our own presentations. It's true. One of the major reasons for objections or stalls is due to the salesperson creating them. What's crazy is most sales representatives don't even realize that this has happened. What I mean is, we failed to handle our most common objections during our pitch, and/or created an objection by not showing our customer that we were the expert in our industry. Hmm, yep, I've been there and done this and created objections where normally there wouldn't have been one. Keep reading—we'll discuss later.

Step 7: Referrals

Can I produce referrals based solely on me? OF COURSE! I built my first and second company based almost exclusively on referrals! I sold my companies, and we generated a lot of sales via referrals. A fact to understand: If your customers don't believe in YOU, then YOU can **NOT** generate a lot of referrals! Referrals are usually the easiest and best method to gain new customers, which equals new sales! Referrals are based on absolute trust!

Okay, so how does one believe in you enough to tell another person, "Hey, talk to so-and-so about such and such"?

Well, you must do all of what we've discussed above, in a manner that your customer not only feels completely satisfied but also feels willing to tell others about you and your company. Your customers **MUST** absolutely believe in **YOU**! We live in a world today where knowledge and social media is only a few keystrokes away on a computer, phone, or tablet. Customers have the ability to provide reviews online about you and your company. If you take care of your customers properly, this can help you immensely in regard to referrals. If you want the referrals, then provide the best customer service you can, so your satisfied customers hopefully provide you with the best reviews and recommendations. This should lead you to more business. You better understand this and make yourself a promise to take care of your customers. Too many sales representatives seek the quick dollar yet fail to understand the ability to make even more money via referrals. Take care of your customers because you **WANT** to, not because you want a quick sale! Think about the future sales via referrals. Customers are savvy—they can sniff out a fake! Be real and take pride in doing a great job for your customers! Yes, it's important to repeat this!

Chapter Three

Sales Education

I'm only here until something else better comes along!

So, are you here for a sales education or are you here until something else better comes along? Guess what... If you're reading this book, congratulations on your **NEW** career field!

If you stumbled into sales, thinking, "Maybe I can do this while I get my degree," or "until I meet someone who can open a door for me in such-and-such career field"—hey, I know that feeling. I've seen it numerous times. It's okay.

What I'm saying is this: Your life is your life. You need to make decisions based on how you prefer to live your life. However, if you're reading this book and are in sales as a temporary or permanent career field, do you want to make minimum wage or would you like to maximize your income?

Minimum wage workers: keep this book in case you need to burn it to keep warm.

The rest of you keep reading. I promise you this: "I may or may not teach you anything new, but I just might teach you what you already knew and weren't using properly." —ME!

Okay, so how does one go about getting an education in sales? Well, it's a tough road full of learning, applying, evaluating, and hard knocks, then learning and applying all over again. What do we need to learn? I'll cover what you need to learn in a broad spectrum in this book. Apply? Are you telling me I need to actually use this information in the real world? If you want to make money, then YES! This isn't for some grade. This is to put money in your bank account!

The important parts of sales go like this:

    1. Knowledge of products and services.

2. Communication between you and the customer.

3. Needs and wants matching.

4. Trial closing. (This should be performed all the way through the sales process; I'll discuss this again later on.)

5. Closing the sale.

6. Referrals.

Already looking a little repetitious? I did mention this. I also mentioned I wouldn't repeat the way many other books do. However, certain areas definitely deserve discussing again and again. Hopefully, I'm not as bland as some of the other books out there! Let's get back to our discussion on sales.

How well do you know your product and service, and how well can you explain it to your customers? Numerous sales industries sell intangibles, such as insurance, pest control, stocks, etc. If what you sell isn't available to be touched or viewed by your customer, can you explain and paint a picture that the customer can visualize clearly? If you sell something your customer can see, touch, smell, etc., can you separate yourself from those who offer a similar product? Such as retail sales, real estate, the automotive world, etc.

You should not only learn the ins and outs of your product or service but believe in it as well. If you yourself don't believe in it, don't sell it. If you do believe in it, which you should, ask yourself this: "Will this product or service help?" If that doesn't fit for you, try this: "Does my customer have a need for my product or service?" If you do **NOT** believe in what you're selling, how can your customer? Do **NOT** sell crap! Believe in what you do and sell what you believe in! I know, I just said this several times within the same paragraph! Sounds pretty important, especially if I repeat in the same paragraph, don't you think? Okay, check this out.

Sometimes your customers have a need for your service, but either they might not want to buy it, or feel as though they might not need it at the current moment. In these situations, the professional salesperson can discover this, and through effective communication, can educate their customers in order to generate the sale. However, what if the same product is being offered by others? Can you separate yourself from the competition? You may need to look at warranty differences, or as a last resort, price. Remember, price is a direct reflection of the value you build. You do **NOT** have to be the cheapest, especially if you deliver the best product or service! Sell value, meaning best products or service at a fair rate for both your customer and your company! Believe in what you do!

How do you differ from your competitors? Can you explain these differences to your customer? This is vital! Most industries have numerous competitors selling very similar products or services. How you separate yourself from the pack is equally important to obtaining a sale, as is what you actually sell. Let's say your price is higher than your competitors for what you're selling. Are you selling the **EXACT** same product or service? What about if your price is different and product is the same? If your product is the same, how do you make up the difference in price? Is it customer service? Guarantee? Free shipping? Are you the cheapest? Etc. Find out that information and then use it to your advantage! It might surprise you how many customers will pay a higher price based on the salesperson, company reputation, or guarantee, even though the product is the same. What I mean is, don't sell yourself short. Yet don't take advantage of your customer, either. Remember, referrals!

Sometimes the best education comes from outside our own company. I ask my sales representatives to call other companies in our industry and allow those company reps to pitch them on what we all sell. I ask them to contact the whole spectrum, from the largest to the local company, which in turn provides a broad spectrum of competition knowledge related to our industry. You should do the same. This allows you to not only learn your industry, but to help you become an expert. What you do is act as if you have no industry knowledge so you can hear how they discuss the industry. How do you know what others provide or what they're going to say if you don't research your industry? Armed with this knowledge, you now have an advantage. You know how to separate yourself from the competition while at the same time being truthful about matching your customer's needs and wants to what you offer. Some people may say that this method isn't right, but I say learning all the ins and outs of your industry and what your competition does or doesn't do is perfectly okay, as it helps you excel as an industry expert! In addition, you're helping **YOUR** customer get what they actually need and want, and in the end, that really is our job as a sales professional! After all, we're here to become the best and help others, right?

One of the worst things you can do as a sales representative is to misrepresent a customer, whether unintentional or not. What I mean is that you tell a person that your competition does or doesn't do such and such, when really, they do, or that your product or service does this and that, when it doesn't. It could cost you the sale, and/or make you or your company look bad, even when you weren't trying to do such. Be truthful and do **NOT** bash your competitors! **Bashing a competitor is just bad for business all around.** Remember what I just said! It's BAD BAD BAD! DO NOT BASH! Discussing differences based on facts is **NOT** bashing, and is fair game, but you better know the facts and differences! Study your industry and competition.

I remember back when I first started selling termite protection in Georgia. I was still green behind the ears, but I had studied my products, my contracts, and my competition. I was speaking with this customer, and he kept asking for more information about how our product actually worked to kill termites and how we were different from others. After we went over how the system actually worked, and how we were different from our competition, he looked at me and said, "Sign me up." He told me that out of several companies that he had out to his house, I not only knew what I was talking about, but I didn't try to make up stuff like others had, and he followed that up by telling me he was a biologist who had researched my industry beforehand. He knew my products and how they worked before I arrived. I was truthful to him and he knew that. Also, I never spoke an ill word about my competition, and he respected that. The main thing I did was have an honest, open conversation while listening to him and his needs and wants, and he bought from me. I recommend you do the same!

The dialogue between you and your customer should flow with some ease. You need to build rapport with your customers. To do this, you need to listen to them! Listening is **NOT** hearing what they're saying while trying to build a rebuttal for your next selling point.

Listening involves understanding the words your customers are using, their tone of voice, as well as their body language. This is part of the communication process. Communicating effectively with your customer shows you care about them, which in turn builds trust. It's very difficult to get a YES from someone who doesn't trust you! **Effective communication is an art in its own right.** One of my main teaching points for my sales representatives is about effective communication. I can write an entire book just on this chapter. You can find more information online regarding effective communication. As you get better on the basics of sales, I suggest you study effective communication to make you even better. Remember, this book is about the basics! You need to be the best in the basics and then enhance your skills in other areas.

If you ever want to field test the difference between listening and hearing, have a conversation with your spouse, or significant other, and slip in a word that doesn't belong in the conversation to see if they pick up on it. If they don't pick up on it, they hear you, but aren't listening. Also, you can spot check the former conversation a while later and ask, "So what do you think about what we talked about earlier?" Be vague in order to find out if they retained the information. If they did, then they were paying attention, which is part of listening. This is a basic fundamental of effective listening. Please understand this: **hearing is NOT listening!** Do yourself a favor and learn more about effective communication in order to make more money. Below is an example.

When you were the customer in a sales presentation, did you ever think to yourself, "Yeah, I really don't need this." Yet, the salesperson just keeps going and going like the Energizer Bunny, without realizing that he or she is NEVER getting that sale. The reason: failure to listen and perform a needs and wants matching analysis. This analysis is nothing more than asking a few simple questions regarding your product or service to see if there's an area of opportunity. I know this next sentence will sound crazy, but we all get caught up at some point and forget to ask pertinent questions to see if there's even a need or want available.

"Why would you try to sell a carpet cleaning service to a person who has tile floors?"

Okay, I get that the above is a bit absurd. However, it happens. Most of the time it's so subtle that many salespeople don't even realize that they weren't paying attention to their customers, and that portion of not paying attention could cost them the sale. You have to LISTEN and match NEEDS AND WANTS! **Pay attention, listen, and care about your customer!**

Many people can say they have tons of stuff in their house they didn't need, yet bought it anyway. The main question to ask is: why did they buy what they did? Or, perhaps, the question in your customer's mind might be, "Did I really want this when I said yes?" Remember, this is a need and/or wants analysis that we're trying to match up in order to produce a sale. We're trying to help people buy what they actually need. We're not talking about impulse buying (meaning buying things customers might not really need or want at the current time, but buy just because it looked or sounded good, or it was on sale at that moment). Preying on impulse buyers can lead to buyer's remorse and/or a possible cancellation. **Your MAJOR goal should be to help people; not just figure out a way to make money off of them.** Can you tell that I'm very motivated about helping others versus taking advantage of people? You should be as well! We're talking about a genuine need or want for our product or service. This sentence is VERY important: **We are looking to help people, while generating referrals from customers who trust us!** Yes, this is what you should focus on.

Here's the deal: Take great care of your current customers as it pertains to what they need and want = happy customers who will refer you! (I didn't put that in bold, caps, or underline it, yet it's the most important thing that you **better** do!) That is, if you want to make really good money! Here's the thing about sales: build a relationship with your current customer, take great care of them, and make them feel and believe that you're helping them based on their needs and wants. The people who do this tend to make the most money via referrals, and for the most part tend to be happier. **Do it because you want to.** Follow the previous sentence and you're set to make more money. This is pretty simple, yet often overlooked, especially when asking for referrals! Most sales reps just want to get the sale and get out... Do yourself a favor: develop a relationship with your existing customer base so you can yield more referrals and money.

Some books and people will tell you that the most important part of the sales process is closing the sale. I disagree. The more work you do up front to develop a relationship, while showing your customer how your product or service meets their needs and wants makes closing the sale easier. This is where your focus should be.

Yet when studying sales, the majority of sales books out there still today, while awesome and loaded with great information, tend to focus mostly on closing the sale. **This book is different!** It's focused on being the best on the basics of sales, as well as how to help your customer. Much of this is based on presentation and industry/product knowledge as already discussed. However, we'll discuss closing the sale too, as it's also important.

Closing the sale involves asking for the business, and therefore many assume this is where you need to be the most gifted in your art. I disagree. Please don't get me wrong, closing the sale and asking for the business is important, but without all of the above aforementioned processes, asking for the sale in this day and age is pretty much useless! If you tell someone a price right away, without building value or explaining what it is you do or how you differ from your competition, more often than not, you won't yield a sale—especially if they're getting multiple quotes. Unless you plan to be the absolute cheapest (which someone will always seek to be the cheapest, so don't do that), you need to learn how to present and explain what it is you do different. **Important Note: Price is a direct reflection of the value you have built!** Remember that important note I just stated each and every time you go sell! Do yourself a favor: **BUILD VALUE!**

As I said above, when paying attention to the customer's wants and needs, closing has been one of the easiest parts of sales. Numerous times, customers have asked me how to buy, instead of me having to ask them. Your sole purpose during a sales presentation should be to match need and wants of your customer with what your company has to offer and ask for the business.

Chapter Four

Prospecting

Don't you give ME Leads?

Okay, so already you have an introduction into prospecting via referrals as listed above. Why don't we discuss the art of prospecting in more detail? This seems to be an area where many sales representatives fall short. Yes, I said fall short. Many salespeople, even the best of the best, can get complacent and slightly lazy with inbound company-generated leads. Many sales reps from time to time will stop searching to create their own leads and focus only on what the company generates for them. When you stop looking or trying to create new avenues, you become complacent. When you become complacent, you start to fail!

Above, we discussed prospecting methods. I'd like to give you a correlation tip into prospecting. When prospecting, you should consider 2 things: time, and money. **Time** and **Money** have a direct correlation to each other. What I mean is if your prospecting method is free or relatively inexpensive, it usually requires more time to work that program. If your method generally costs a good bit of money, then chances are your time requirement is lowered, usually because you're paying someone else to spend their time to help generate your leads. The rest of obtaining new business meets somewhere in the gray area between these two of time and money. Look at time and money as being on a seesaw—as one goes up, the other generally goes down. In addition to this, look at your time versus money spent/money made. The question to ask is, in relationship to what you make versus time spent prospecting, are you maximizing your average dollar per hour? What I mean is, how long on average does it take for you to pitch and sign up a new customer and is what you're doing on your own (prospecting) enabling you to achieve that? Consider an average of all your different prices, as well as average out your time based on different pitch times. This will give you your average dollar/hour rate.

According to this seesaw method and/or average dollar per hour rate, we're ready to discuss ways in which to find potential customers, which I refer to as pipelines and fishbowls. Let's discuss.

First off, in order to succeed in sales, you need to have a pipeline or several pipelines from which to extract sales and new business. Pipelines are nothing more than amassing people to talk to, who could turn into a customer or client, and how you find them. Without full pipelines, sales representatives will fail to produce the constant flow of sales, which yields less money in your pocket! We do NOT want that. Generating your pipeline is nothing more than putting your potential customers into a database by category of how you discovered them. When discussing a pipeline, think of a fishbowl—as you keep filling that fishbowl with water it will eventually overflow. This is exactly what I mean by prospecting and pipelines. You **have** to keep finding new people to talk to in order to fill and overflow that fishbowl!

I recommend having numerous pipelines that you work on a consistent basis. This way you never go broke! It's like the old adage says: never put all your eggs in one basket. Some of these pipelines may be season specific. To start, you should work 2 to 3 programs until you become very proficient at all of these programs and then add a new program. When you add the new program, work it until it becomes proficient just like the other programs, but remember, do **NOT** drop the ball on the other programs or you could suffer, meaning potential loss of income.

I challenge you to find customers not listed here. There are always some you can think of that maybe I didn't. Realize what will work for you, **build a plan**, and then make sure you work your plan! Also understand, what works for some may not work for you and vice versa. Why don't we discuss some of the more common methods of finding new customers?

We listed one of the BEST means of producing new customers already: Referrals! Okay, so how do we **GET** referrals? Many different methods are available in which to prospect for referrals. What I'll discuss here is a common method that many, under my guidance, have felt useful. NOTE: Referrals are one of the best methods to raise your income, if you do **NOT** get a lot of referrals, ask yourself why not, and then, please talk to others who do get a lot of referrals. You can also read the following section again and again, as well as practice and fine-tune your craft of obtaining referrals. No kidding, this is super important!

To get referrals, you need to first bring the conversation up, then, usually **AFTER** your customer decides to use your product or service, ask for them. Make sure your customer gets what you've promised, which means some form of follow-up. Remember not to over-promise! Then, through your follow-up, make sure your customer is completely satisfied with your product and/or service. If something doesn't go as planned, help fix it as this goes the extra mile toward gaining a referral as well as keeping a customer for your company. Once all of this is good to go, then you can really start the process of asking for actual referrals. You can bring up the conversation of referrals earlier in the sales process, but here is where you want to ask your satisfied customers for actual referrals.

There are many different ways to ask for a referral. It's up to you and how you feel most comfortable. It can be as simple as, "Mrs. Customer, I thank you very much for trusting us with your business. I provide for my family by being able to help others such as yourself. Once we provide you with the service or product in which you selected and you are satisfied, would you be so kind as to provide me with others that I may help?" It can also be as simple as, "Mr. or Mrs. Customer, thank you for believing in me and my company, may I ask you if there's anyone you know who would benefit from what I do?" Besides referrals, what other ways are there to get new business?

In our modern arena of social media, referrals can be your best friend. You need to utilize social media to the best of your ability. Interact with your customers, as well as potential new customers. Discuss what you have to offer and how it can help your potential customers, yet be respectful of different viewpoints. One thing to note here is, don't sign up a customer and then think you never have to deal with them again. You do this, you lose money and possibly an existing customer!

Well, when it comes to trying to figure out how to get new business, I like to think of it like horse racing. What I mean by this is, when horses line up to race, they have blinders on. This prevents them from seeing the distractions that could prevent them from achieving their desired results. From time to time, you need to wear your blinders, and from time to time you need to take those blinders off so you can evaluate your performance and see new opportunities. Remember this: opportunity is everywhere, it's up to you to find it, and to act upon it!

Okay, so let us discuss avenues of business attainment:

- Referrals
- Social Media
- Business Cards
- Networking
- Door to Door Sales

- Cold Calling

- Canvassing Neighbors (business or personal) of Current Customers

- Flyers

- County Websites for New Business Licenses

- Smaller Scale Ads, such as Community Publications

- City or County Websites

- Banner Ads (such as sports fields)

- Phone Book Ads

- Online Ads

- Billboards

- Company Leads

Please note, this represents a very small-scale version of prospecting. I've found that usually within 30 minutes of brainstorming with a sales team, we find many other avenues in which to gain business. In some respects, my sales teams have been able to list 30 or more ways to generate new customers. The key here is find ways that work for you and make you money, then work those prospecting methods to make the most money you can.

Of the ways listed, how do we make these effective? Let us discuss some of these methods of prospecting.

Business Cards should be professional looking and handed out **EVERYWHERE!** How many times do you walk into a place and they may have their cards sitting out as a take one, but they might not even hand a card out, let alone speak of them? Make a card that's easy for a prospective customer to remember, so they can call YOU and not your competition. I once heard that a successful salesperson should pass out more than 1000 business cards per month. I'm not sure if this is a number that yields success, but what I do know is this: Pass your cards out constantly to prospects who you feel could potentially use your service or product. In addition, share your business cards with those you can network with. Just slinging cards doesn't mean sales, yet hoarding your cards definitely does NOT equal more sales.

The old **Door to Door Sales Method** has gained renewed interest in many companies lately. You should also be aware that when looking for different means of prospecting, the methods will most likely change from time to time. The door to door, or door knocking, with the evolution of the DO NOT CALL LIST has picked up speed in the last couple of years. This method requires a ton of time, sweat, and some very thick skin, as you will most definitely get a lot of **NO's** in many various ways. Even though you'll get more NO's than YES's, and it can be time consuming, this method can also be very prosperous. This method is for both business to business and residential customers.

Cold Calling can be performed in several different ways. Cold calling in general can be classified as picking up the phone and dialing someone or a business out of the blue to see if there's an interest in your product or service. Again, this method will require a ton of time, sweat and really, really thick skin. Hang in there, and remember: learn and apply, learn and apply! There are different degrees of cold calling. For example, you can warm up a cold call by sending a form of correspondence first, such as a flyer. Again, expect more NO's than Yes's. This method can also be very lucrative.

One of the best ways that worked for me when I was out in the field selling, whether I was selling to residential customers, or selling businesses, was **canvassing**. I would leverage my customers in a particular area to help me get new sales in that same area. Many of the potential customers would either know or have heard of the customer I referenced, and it would "warm" that person up some so that they would talk with me. Many times, I would end up with a new customer, maybe not the same day, but with good follow-up it did. If I was selling to businesses, I would talk with every business in a shopping center, and let them know who I was and what I offered, and yes I left a business card even if I knew they were going to throw it away. After all, we ARE creatures of habit! I recommend asking your current customers for permission to use their name or company as one of your clients. Once given permission, my current customers knew I would be promoting their business as I was seeking new business for myself, and if the presentation was getting a little tough, I would say, "Why don't you ask (customer x) down the street how well we take care of them?" Sometimes I would get them to call while I was there, others I would schedule a time for me to follow up at a later date. This would allow them time to check us out at their leisure. I made a lot of sales this way! In fact, this is one of the main methods of how I **really** started growing my own company.

Flyers are a decent way of advertising. Usually, flyers are relatively inexpensive but require a great deal of time to put where people can come in contact with them. I spent quite a bit of time doing flyers. I had some places where I would put them, and some areas they probably ended up in the trash, yet some areas were gold mines for me. You have to really work this program on a consistent basis for it to pay off. What I mean is if you put out a bunch of flyers and then expect people to call you for your business, you're wrong. If you think you can put out your flyers, and they're going to stay there until the end of time, think again! You need to know your flyer placement locations, and you need to check up on them quite often. If you know they're being thrown away, find somewhere else to put them. If your potential customer can't find you, how can they do business with you?

We discussed a few ways to prospect new customers. I challenge you to find what works best for you, and to eventually work many programs and build up several different pipelines, so you can reach your desired level of success.

Networking is another major source of income. Either get involved with a networking group or do your own. What I mean by doing your own is, find businesses that are in your wheelhouse and ask to trade cards and network together. They hand out yours as needed and you hand out theirs as needed.

Chapter Five

One Call That's All, Right?

It's never just one call! I skipped over the presentation portion of this exercise because most companies usually have their own way of presenting their products or services, and you should learn the presentation in their way.

Okay, so you've generated some leads via prospecting, or your company has graced you with their precious leads. Yes, I said precious. Your company spent time, energy, and/or money bringing these leads in, and if you're lucky enough to receive them, then treat them as if they are a precious commodity!

It's important to note that not every sale is closed on the first meeting. Some of my best sales come from either multiple meetings or several phone calls. This is called follow-up. I cannot stress enough how important follow-up is. If you want to be broke, do NOT follow up!

Successful salespeople will often tell you what I'm going to tell you, and that is, most of my sales actually stem from following up with my customers. Many times, customers just aren't ready to make a final decision at the first meeting. Sometimes, they need to check over their budget, or perhaps it could be a timing issue. Follow-up gives the customer the ability to figure out their timeline or financial position, as well as giving them a chance to see if you really care.

Yes, sometimes customers won't make the final decision at the first meeting simply because they want to see how well you'll take care of them. Following up is a way that shows care to your new customer. The reason for this, many times, is that savvy customers who consistently receive sales calls are busy with their own agenda, and to put you off to another day and time is a way for them to weed out the people they don't wish to do business with. Getting back in touch with them at a specified time or date that works for their schedule allows you to stand out from many others, and in a lot of cases you end up with business.

How do we perform this follow-up process? Well, that can be an art all in its own right. Sometimes it requires phone calls; sometimes it might be an additional meeting. The best way I've found to follow up is to ask your potential customer for permission to either call them, or to schedule another meeting. Without their consent, you could be bugging them, which could turn them off from using you and your company, period.

So, how do we get permission? Depending on my customer and their needs and wants, and after possibly trying to close the sale several times, I simply ask, "Mr. / Mrs. Customer, I understand you need some time to make your final decision. When would be a convenient time for me to contact you, to see how things are going?"

When your customer gives you a date and time to follow up, then follow up at that specific date and time. Don't wait until later, or you could end up losing the sale. Also, when you're following up, tell your customer you're following up based on your previous discussion. If no decision has been made about the outcome of your presentation yet, then ask to schedule an additional follow-up date and time.

Chapter Six

Sales Numbers

What are those?

Okay so we've talked about prospecting and follow-up, what on Earth are we talking about when we mention sales numbers? Actually, this subject should be one of the most used, yet easily understood subjects of this whole book, if you do math correctly.

So, what are we talking about, commission rates?

Um, no.

We are talking about how we figure out how much money we can make in a given period of time, based on our skills.

Okay, so first off, you need to take a look at what your average sale in your industry equals. Then, take your average to the lowest commission rate your company offers and apply it to the sale. This will give you a bottom-line dollar amount that you can expect to earn should you follow your company's formula and generate sales.

Example: if your company offers 10% commission on a sale, and you make a $1000 sale, you earn $100.

If your company has a tier system, continue to use the bottom tier as a baseline until you're more acquainted with your normal sales volume per month. Also, if you can bonus extra commission percentages based on package deals, or volumes, or total sales dollars, then use that just as that—a bonus! The reason being is you want to basically dumb down/simplify the lowest amount you can make via your sales in order to build a plan or goal, and anything above that, consider a bonus. This way you know exactly what you need to do in order to make what you need or want in terms of income, and any amount over that plan or goal equals extra money in your bank account—aka bonus.

When trying to figure your sales figures or goals for each month, be realistic! If you normally sell $20,000 a month, why base your figures on $100,000? Don't try to impress the boss with a big number you're not going to deliver, unless of course you know you can! Make your numbers tough yet attainable. Many sales representatives fail because they shoot for the stars without a realistic plan, and many have no plan at all, but that's a whole different subject. If you make weak and easy numbers that you definitely know you can do, you won't push yourself to achieve the things you actually could. Likewise, if you make them unattainable, most of you will quit trying to achieve them, and then you'll fall right back into mediocrity.

So how do we determine our goals? Well, for one start with your monthly/annual goal or budget and work backwards all the way down to what it is you need to do each day to achieve that monthly/annual goal or budget. Here's what I mean. Say your annual goal is $120,000 in new sales; divide that by 12 months, which equals $10,000 per month. Take the number or days you work per month and divide that into your monthly goal. That equals what you need to do each working day. So if, you average 20 working days in a normal month (Monday – Friday) then 20 / $10,000 = $500 per working day average sales day. Find what you need to do to make at least $500 per day in sales revenue. I used these numbers just for simple math, but you get the point.

One very very important note: allow some room for failure! If you need $500 per working day and you know you may have days where no sales are made (prospecting doesn't always lead to a sale) then allow for a couple of zeros but offset that with days above $500 a day. What I mean is this (as an example only), up your daily sales needs to $750 for 4 days out of the month, and $500 for the other 16 days, which will allow you to have 2 days of no sales at all. This accounts for failure, which as sales professionals we know we don't always sell something every single day even though we try. In this formula, you target those bigger goals first, and then if you have a zero day, it's okay, because you adjusted and calculated for it. You can still reach your goal because 4 days at $750 plus 14 days at $500 and 2 days at $0 equals $10,000 in sales which was the original goal. Make sense?

Depending on what type of sales profession you're in depends on how you build your goals or budgets. No matter what field you sell in, we all have to do this to some degree if we want to be successful! What I'm providing is a baseline model by which you can adjust accordingly with your field.

Working in this part of the program can change everything! If you want to take the wife on a special vacation, but need extra funds for it, well just increase your daily needs to offset the price of that vacation. You can work smarter and sometimes a little harder yet make a tremendous amount more.

Example: I need to buy a new car. I usually sell $30,000 a month for my company at 10% commission. I need to sell more to cover the expense of a $30,000 car, which usually yields a $600 - $700 car payment. Okay no problem, $30,000 a month at 10% = $3000 a month in pay. So, we need an additional $1000 a month in pay (taxes and easy math) on a 20 workday month, how do I achieve this? Let's say our average sale is $2500, which normally makes us 12 sales per month. We would need to increase our monthly sales by 4 per month, which is once per week. It gets more complicated than this but not much more, so we'll keep it simple for a minute and explain the complicated later.

Based on your closing ratio (which is what I meant by more complicated) you take the number of sales you need to be in excess of your normal monthly total and divide by your closing ratio. This equals how many more proposals you need to make to yield those additional sales. The national closing average of salespeople is around 25% closing ratio (due to prospecting and that most salespeople don't study their trade). So, let's assume the 25% ratio of proposals to sales and apply it to our current formula. If we need 4 more sales to cover the cost of our new $30,000 car, we take 4 / 25% = 16 new proposals (remember, this is an average). So basically, if we want to buy that new car and not feel the burden of its cost, then we need to find 16 new qualified prospects to propose which on a 25% closing ratio should yield 4 additional sales per month.

Yes, this is the average, I currently close between 60-70% depending on the month (I was in the pest control industry, and it's seasonal). Your ratios will depend on how well you not only learn about your industry, but also improve your sales, meaning cycles and timeline of how long it takes to close a deal, plus your education levels.

The important part of this subject is you must find your formula and work on it!

Chapter Seven

Effective Communication

This section is extremely important! If you don't learn this subject, you'll sell yourself short! No kidding, this is definitely one section that will separate you from mediocre sales reps. Communication is vital! This is going to be a crash course into effective communication, meaning Google this subject and learn it more in depth than what I'm teaching. It's very important if you want to make really good money! If you only remember one thing, effective communication is it! It tells you more than anything else I've written! It helps improve closing percentages, which means more money!

You need to read body language and listen effectively, so you know what your customers want. Then match their wants and needs with what you offer in a manner that guides them to potentially say yes.

Pay attention to non-verbals, mostly told in body language, but also in tone of voice, how are they sitting/standing.

When performing your presentation, make sure you're using proper tone of voice, voice inflections at correct spots, correct body language, and mirror your customer. So many times, when I speak with people outside of a sales proposal, they speak in a normal conversation, but then when it's time to sell, they turn into what I call the sales robot.

What I mean is this, if your customer is sitting up, listening attentively, don't sit back and go monotone into robot salesperson mode! Mirror your customer by sitting up attentively and speaking assertively and being fairly excited about what you do. Have a normal conversation with your customer just as you would with a friend or colleague.

Effective communication is one of the most important things you can do for your business. Not just for sales, but for service and admin as well. This, when done properly, keeps current customers from canceling based on a lower price, and for sales makes it easier for your potential customer to say YES. **Your customer believes you when you are excited about what you do and also when you believe in what you do!**

Again, just have a normal conversation, listen and understand what your potential customer is saying to you, and discuss what you have to offer. Read body language because that will tell you more than what your customer is actually saying.

Example: if your customer is saying yes, but is sitting back with folded arms, they are most likely saying no!

You still need to funnel the conversation, by staying in charge of the conversation while at the same time making your customer feel either at ease or in charge. This is **NOT** a gimmick to trick them, it's merely a way to figure out how to get them involved in the conversation! You need to understand that the final decision is **ULTIMATELY** up to your customer, and you're there to help them.

Ask trial closing questions, such as, does that make sense? Fair enough? Okay? Right?

You want to make sure you're getting yes answers when asking these. If not, DO NOT PROCEED. Ask more questions to find out what the customer is unsure of, answer that area or you'll end up with an objection that goes back to whatever area you lost them at. Understand your customer may or may not tell you that, so you may need to ask probing questions to get them to speak about it in more than just a yes or no answer.

If **NOT**, you could end up with a stall like, "I need to think about it" versus them saying, "Well I really didn't understand what you were discussing."

The better you are at effective communication, and caring about doing the best to match needs and wants for your customer, the more they'll recognize this, and more people will say yes to you!

Chapter Eight

Goals

Many salespeople talk about goals, but as they talk, they fail to plan. Making a well-defined plan is the absolute key to success. Many books have been written just on this subject alone. So, let's discuss goals and how important goals are as they relate to sales. Here we'll touch not only on goals, but how to align our goals with our plan for sales in order to maximize our efficiency and effectiveness.

One can say, "Okay I want to be the best," yet fail to plan or align goals to reach the final destination. This happens a lot in sales. Good intentions do **NOT** equal good results! You must build some kind of plan. Example: watch a new sales representative who is graduating from training and going into the field on his or her own for first time alone. They are confident, and try hard, but without a well-defined plan and great leadership, as time passes, confidence drains, and eventually they find many excuses or reasons to leave.

I'm not here to make you some sort of magic formula to reach riches for you. What I'm writing about is the basic formulas to help grow your business and help you reach your goals! I want you to make good money! With properly defined goals you can build a plan that allows you to maximize your efforts.

Goals for the most part are intangible as it relates to sales. What I mean by this is, sales depends on how many customers say yes, how well you know your products or services, and how well you can build a relationship and correlate with your customers. However, goals are definitely measurable, meaning you can see day to day, week to week, month to month, and year to year, to determine if you're on track to meet or exceed your own expectations. Yet, as it relates to goals, you can't taste, touch, or smell goals. What you can do is see if you're on track to reach your goals if you have a well-defined plan. You must set a well-defined plan that's realistic for you to achieve. You can build a sales plan, similar to a business plan, to track your progress, in order to see what your closing percentage is, to see how many people you need to talk to yield one sale, and figure out how many sales you need to make your desired amount of income. Planning will help you understand how many people on average you need to talk to daily in order to reach your goals.

Visualize this: if you don't set goals, you'll end up like tumbleweeds being blown around in the wind, meaning you wander aimlessly on your quest for sales without ever reaching your full potential. Don't be a tumbleweed—set goals and build a plan to achieve those goals!

It's vital to look into the mirror and set realistic goals. You need to ask, what is it I can really achieve? Be sincere, don't lie to yourself! All you need to do is be realistic and then aim a little higher. Then read this book again, as well as other books so you can learn even more and become even better at sales to yield even better results which equate to more money in your bank account. Most sales representatives who don't last tend to make unrealistic goals or budgets, then make excessive excuses as to why they can **NOT** meet these goals or budgets. Don't become one of those sales representative statistics!

How do we set a well-defined plan? (We MUST look at realistic goals) How about we look at an example below. I discussed some of these above, but let's look at this again more in depth as it's vital to success.

First, you need to look at your commission rates and determine an average (this is based on what you sell across all mediums). You may have several different products or services and thus may need to make an average for each. Let's take your commission rate versus average sale to determine your average dollar rate per sale. (This is what you make per sale depending on product or service). Then, let's look at how much you'd like to make per year via income.

We then take what you want to make and do the math for what your average commission rate is per sale to determine what you need to sell for the year. Remember this: we're building a roadmap to success for you to follow, and without a map it's very easy to get lost.

Again, look at the annual need to have/want to have income. This is your major goal for the year and should be done each year. Once you establish what you want to make per year (major goals), we then work backwards to break this income down into attainable amounts per month. We must break this major goal down into smaller amounts to make it easier for you to accomplish your smaller goals that are aligned with your major goal via your roadmap to success. Let's look at the smaller goals.

So, we just talked about annual goals and annual income while touching on breaking those goals down into smaller increments. One thing we also need to consider is variable income from variable months. Meaning, do you have certain times of the year where sales peak higher than the rest of the year? Here you want to make an average, and anything over that average, leave your bank account as a bonus. This will help should you have months where income is less, or if you have a sales job where during certain seasons, your income is generally higher/lower than other times. This helps balance your month to month pay over the course of a year.

Goals should be viewed as a measuring tool, **NOT** as an absolute must achieve! You need to define your end result which equals your goals but then break them down into smaller more attainable results. One thing that is **VERY** important to note is, when selling, you must allow for a NO SALES DAY! What I mean is, you won't sell your average every day. It's an average for a reason! Use your plan accordingly to get sales and do your best to get those sales as soon as you can but allow yourself a day or two where you might not sell anything. This will help keep your morale up, plus allow you to stay on track to reach your monthly and annual sales goals. Remember this: NO one sells everything all the time!

Okay, so we set some goals, now what do we do, how do we achieve our goals, and what are we talking about?

Let's discuss a well-defined plan. We need to define what we're selling, and an average of how long it takes to make a sale. Depending on what business you're in, your sales formula can vary, as well as the length of time to close a sale, and sales price. This is why we need to determine an average.

Now, we need to build a plan based on our goals while considering our commission rate from our average sale. In addition, we need to consider how many people we need to solicit and how many people are willing to say yes based on our abilities (our closing percentage). This gives us our formulas to work backwards from average commission to how many proposals we need to do each day, and how many people we need to talk to or see each day to get one real proposal.

Proposals, yes, we MUST track and follow up on these! Who likes to work for free? NOT me! So, we have to track this info. You need to track your closing percentages as well. When looking at closing percentages, make sure you're honest with yourself, because if you try to make them look better than they really are, you're only messing with yourself, and your sales managers. YES, I've seen people try to make their numbers and percentages look better so their bosses leave them alone. However, this doesn't help you with your plan, nor does it help you get to your desired goals. Know this: if you have a sales manager who actually cares about his or her team, their job is to actually work for and help you achieve **your goals**, not theirs! So, be realistic with yourself! Keep this info in a database if that's what your company asks, or at the very least keep it on a note pad (the old school way).

Follow-up is paramount, and one of the MOST important things you can do for yourself and your company in regard to sales. Look at it this way: if you cold call a business or person, pitch your sales and they don't buy on the spot, yet you fail to follow up, you just wasted your time and your company's time. In addition to wasting all that time, you as a sales representative, actually ended up working for FREE! **Who in the world wants to work for FREE?**

Sounds pretty simple and basic, right? It really is, but most people in sales fail to do this. The top money making people in your company have some sort of plan, goals, or tracking system in order for them to stay on top and make really good money—go ask them about it. You should have a system in place too! Following up on existing proposals is one area that can really separate the decent from the great! If I had to estimate where most of my sales come from, the answer is going to be from following up with customers I already met with and proposed. Remember, if you do NOT follow up with those who needed more time or were set on getting other quotes, the answer most often is NO, and you just left good money on the table for some other salesperson to collect!

We just discussed having a plan and follow-up. Now, let us look at an example of what I'm talking about via goals and a plan to achieve those goals. We'll use simple numbers for this.

Say you'd like to make $120,000.00 a year, which is your annual goal. How do we get there? We must break it down into smaller chunks to make it achievable, meaning form a well-defined plan. First, we divide the $120,000 by 12 months which equals $10,000 a month. It looks a little easier already, right? Okay, let's break that down even further. Divide $10,000 by 4 (average number of weeks per month) which means you basically need to make $2500 per week. Take a 5 day work week and break it down one more time and you need to make $500 per day in commissions. Depending on what you're selling, average sales price, and your sales pitch to close cycle (overall closing percentage), all of this will depend on how much activity you need to do to generate one sale (prospecting).

In addition, you need to look at what you're selling, meaning, is there a part of the year that has a super busy season yet slows down in other seasons? If so, you may need to adjust your monthly goals and/or activity to reflect these trends. What I mean is, maybe you have to increase your daily and weekly goals during your busier times and give yourself a smaller goal budget through the slower times.

Now that we've discussed how much you want to make per year and how to break that down into smaller amounts, let's discuss how we get there. This is where planning is paramount but understand that sales are an ever evolving career field where circumstances constantly change. So, you need to be ready to change as well, in order to stay on top.

As stated above, you need to take your normal average sale and times that by your commission rate for the average sale to determine your average pay from these sales. I say normal because you'll have some sales that exceed the normal rates, and you'll have some sales that are smaller than normal.

Then take your daily sales goal (as determined by your plan) and divide it by the average sales commission rate you're paid. From there, you need to look at your closing percentage, meaning what percentage rate of the customers you pitch, do you actually end up with a sale from. Be honest! Anyone can fix their numbers to look great, but it won't help you achieve your goals! This number will tell you how many customers need to say yes to you and actually purchase what you're selling.

Then, look at how many people that you have to share your knowledge and expertise with (pitch) to yield one sale, and that will give you the number of presentations you need to perform on a given day. It's important to note you may need to look at how many times you have to meet or talk with your potential customers to yield that sale as not all sales jobs are completed in just one meeting (phone or in person).

Once you determine how many presentations you need to perform in a given day to yield one sale, you need to figure out how many people, on average, you need to talk to in a given day to yield one presentation.

Once you have an average number of people you need to talk to give one presentation, make **THAT** you daily goal! One thing to realize is that numbers change, customers change, and those daily goals may change as well. What I mean is some days and, in some months, you may need to see and talk to more people to achieve your daily or monthly sales goal. Also, in some months, during peak sales cycles, you may need to see and/or speak with less people. Key thing to remember: **Adjust as Necessary!** Another part to understand is, as you get better and better at all of what I'm sharing with you, your closing ratios will go up, and the number of people you need to talk to, to make one sale will go down. Do NOT slow down just because that ratio gets better, keep working hard and smarter, as this will yield even more money in your bank account!

So we've discussed goals, and plans according to doing business, but I'd also like to discuss how this helps on the home front in your personal lives. You also need to make goals and plans in your personal life. Many of these can and should be aligned with your business goals or plan. Let me give you an example of what I'm talking about.

Say you're making x number of dollars a month, but you really would like to take your significant other or family on a really nice vacation, or maybe you want a new car, or maybe you want to do a major upgrade to your house. Perhaps, you want to do all of the above. For the sake of this book, let's say what you're currently making in sales covers all your bills and leaves a little extra left over, but not enough left over to do the things I stated above. How do we get those things above too? How do we excel in sales so we can make more income?

Well, you set a little higher goal, build a well-defined plan to achieve that goal, and then work it so you achieve that goal. This way, you make that extra money on your paycheck while still being able to afford your normal lifestyle. One of the greatest parts about sales is being able to make as much money as you'd like, based on how hard you're willing to work, as well as, who wants to pay the most for your services, based your abilities! That last part, based on your abilities, **depends completely on you, your knowledge of sales, and your work ethic!** Want to make the most money? If so, learn everything you can, and put it to good use! You don't have to work the most hours to make the most money in sales, but you do need to be educated and diligent in your work ethic. Remember, it's not always about harder, but more about smarter!

Goals and well-defined plans can and often do go hand in hand with your business and personal life, and you should take this into account, because more often than not, it helps motivate you to achieve your goals!

Chapter Nine

The Basics?

Really, Should I Master These?

To answer this question in its simplest form, YES! Many books, sales teachers, mentors, and great sales managers will tell you that the difference between the elite and the mediocre is the ability to master the basics.

Think of the elite, and if you want to be elite, take this to heart. The elite study the basics and then they constantly revisit the basics often. What the best of the best do (elite) is fine-tune their skills. They evaluate themselves, figure out the areas they need to improve, and then work to improve those areas until those areas become a positive strength versus one of their weaknesses. Think of professional sports for this topic. Professional athletes spend most of their time honing all aspects of their craft. You should do this also if you want to be the best and make the kind of money you set in your goals. The reason the top performers, or elite, do this is simple. They know that if they don't constantly practice the basics and fine-tune their skills, they can fall off course very easy, and as such end up eventually making less money than they did. Sales is a world of constant studying and applying.

I for one, read this book often. Yeah, I know I'm writing it, but I also still sell. So, when I feel like I'm not performing to my maximum, I read my own book again and again, and it helps to put me back on the highway of success. I hope it does the same for you!

I remember sitting in a few Brian Tracy seminars, and to somewhat paraphrase him, we can either travel the road unknown, or we can actually travel the interstate with GPS, in order to achieve our goals and get where we want to go. He didn't speak those actual words, but I am. What I mean by this, is this: as sales professionals, we can just run the leads our company provides us and follow unknown back roads, or we can have clear cut set goals of what WE want to accomplish for our families and then build a path to achieve those goals which equals the interstate and success.

Another gentleman, a preacher once said, we can have a goal of getting to Miami, however, if we get on I-95 North without direction and a plan, we will NEVER get to Miami!

It's amazing to me how easy that sounds, on getting to Miami, yet how difficult it becomes when we apply it to our own lives and sales!

Being on the interstate to me means this: the ability to close as many sales as possible in the shortest time available, while creating referrals and additional prospects along the way, which yields future sales and clients.

In order to do this, you better become an expert on the basics, which enables you to maximize what I just said. Okay, let us discuss what the basics are so you can be the best you can!

1. **Know your product or service, and your company.**

2. **Understand your customers' needs and wants.**

3. **Provide your knowledge effectively to your prospect in manner that exudes confidence.**

4. **Have the ability to sell on difference rather than price.**

5. **Know your competition and have the ability to discuss without bashing the competition. (No one likes to be bashed; one, and two, it makes you look bad! Do NOT bash!)**

In order to be the master, one needs to learn. For all of us out there selling, we need to constantly train ourselves. In a world where sales are so vitally important, sales training lacks, when this should be one of the most highly sought after training empires around. Do you really want to become a master? Well, if so, you had better take up the art of self-study.

You need to be able to look at yourself in the mirror and evaluate your strengths and weaknesses. Write these down, and once you've determined the weaknesses that are holding you back from making more sales, pick one to work on, and bring it to a position of strength. Then, re-evaluate, and correct the weakest link again. Do this over and over again and you'll find yourself in the world of top performers! We'll only be as good as our weakest link! What I mean is this: if you can pitch the sale but are weak in closing, you'll close fewer sales. If you study, bring that closing weakness to a position of strength, you'll close more sales without having to make any more proposals. This will yield more money to your paycheck. This same information can be found in just any sales book or guide. It's completely up to you as to what you do with this information. I for one like making big dollars, and therefore research and learn better ways to work smarter, and harder to make that happen. Now, how do we close sales when people start opposing us?

Chapter Ten

Objections?

You Can't Sell Stupid!

Whoa? What, people don't sign up the minute we finish our presentation? Okay, some do if you're good or they did their research and were going to buy already! BUT, what about those who are undecided? How do we help them say yes? Please note I said HELP versus coax or coerce!

Yes, many of your prospects will need extra time to make that final decision of yes. It's up to you as a professional to determine what is what. I've had many customers sitting on what I call the fence waiting for a little extra guidance to say hey it's okay to buy from me and my company. Also, I've had tons of customers who needed to either look at their finances or talk with their spouses before making a final decision. Which by the way leads us back to following up!

Do NOT be afraid of hearing an objection. Many objections are just a sign of hey I didn't explain something entirely. If you know your most common objections, then you should learn how to lay them down and overcome them BEFORE they ever come up! We'll discuss some in a little while.

Objections also should be welcomed to a point. Many times, if you covered all your bases there shouldn't be but a few objections, or only one.

Price is NOT always an objection if you've read and understood this book! Price is a direct reflection of value built with your prospect versus service or product offered.

Objections should be welcomed, as it sometimes tells you where to focus your presentation and build that value you may have missed.

When handling objections, you need to be aware of your customer's beliefs and feelings and not offend your potential customer.

Okay, so what is an objection? Also, we'll discuss stalls, or what I call false objections.

Objections are this: they are a way of telling you that a customer is interested but needs more information on a certain portion of your presentation to help them buy.

It could be that your prospect just needs clarification about how you intend to satisfy their purchase, such as, "Will my family benefit from your service or product?" Also, it could mean, hey, I was stuck in an earlier part of your presentation when you were talking about this or that.

Your job is to figure out through discussion, what their concern is, and how best to overcome it.

Objections are NOT price related! On a rare occasion, price is the main issue, but normally that equates to a stall! When I hear price is the main objection, often it relates to not enough value built for the customer to see it.

Here are a few stalls: price too high, need to talk to spouse (although this can actually be real, but it's most often a stall), getting other quotes, need to think about it, etc.

You MUST be careful when dealing with a stall because it can lead to a NO sale. Objections, most often when treated correctly, can be overcome and lead to a sale.

How do you decipher what a stall versus an objection is? Well, you have to tread lightly but ask a few questions to figure out which is which. A lot of times people will throw out the stall in order to avoid giving up their real objection in hopes of not having to say YES on the spot (on the spot doesn't always mean on the first pitch!)

Example: Say you're selling napkins to a food establishment, and they put out what looks like an objection of, "Well let me think about it and get back to you." Most often that's a stall rather than an objection, but you must be careful in your navigation of handling that. You might reply, "That's fine, but let me ask you this, does your current company do....?"

Another: Let's say you already asked if they needed to discuss this with another person(s), and they said NO, but getting towards your closing they say, "Let me discuss this with my partner"—it's a STALL! You then refer politely back to the part where you asked this question. Again, be nice and professional or you'll lose the sale! You might ask, "Earlier when we were discussing the final decision and if others needed to make this decision with you, you said you could do this, is it about the price or the service or product that's holding you up?"

Example of a real objection: "I like what you're saying but I'm not sure I think that drilling my front porch for termites is necessary." You could reply, "I understand how you might think that, however, studies from many universities have shown that termites most often travel between expansion joints from concrete slabs poured at different times and therefore we need to treat that area in order to keep them out of your home, wouldn't you agree?"

Another one: "I see what you're saying, but the other company said I would be okay with cola boxes every 2 months." Your reply: "I understand, however, in our discussion, you told me you were going through X number of boxes per month. According to our conversation, your current cola box setup, and looking around your restaurant, you don't have enough room to store additional boxes. Wouldn't our coming out monthly suit your needs better?"

One more to give you a third look: "I need to discuss this with my spouse/business partner." WOW! Yeah, that one stumps even the elite sales pros! Why? Because it can be true, but it can also be a stall. You need to ask a few probing questions to figure out which is which, and had you asked these questions way back in the beginning they may have told you which was which. Meaning, in your initial conversation to setup an appointment, if you asked, "Would there be anyone else you need to consult with in order to choose our service" (or any other more polite way of doing that) they most likely would have told you! The major key for this is to find out if you're dealing with the actual decision maker, a partner, or are you going through a gate keeper set up by the owner to keep salespeople out!

Well, dang, you didn't even tell me how to find out who is who! There are some techniques to find out what is what and who is who. From industry to industry, it varies, and you need to learn those most likely from your boss or colleagues.

While one of the most widely used methods of overcoming objections is the feel, felt, found method, I highly discourage that practice! It's **SO** 80's and 90's of sales and people are WAY smarter these days! However, I do recommend using some variation of that method. For instance, instead of saying "I know how you feel, but others buying this same type of car felt the same way and have found..." You might change it up to "I understand what you're saying, can I ask you a question?" Or another version: "So what you're telling me is that... and based on... you would prefer..."

OBJECTIONS?

You have a good idea of what I'm talking about, but I'm not going to give you all the normal objection responses in this book. Why? Because they change constantly from industry to industry.

Here's what I will tell you about objections: 1. Welcome them! 2. Figure out what your most common objections are in your industry. 3. Learn how to present your product or service in a manner that overcomes the most common objections in your industry before they pop up, and 4. The objections that still pop up ask probing questions that provoke an open ended answer rather than just a yes answer. Meaning engage your customer in regular conversation!

You can ask questions that steer a customer into a yes/no answer, which I refer to as a yes set question. OR you can ask open ended question that require a longer answer. I prefer more often than not the open ended questions! Many sales books say do this in the beginning, of which I agree. The quicker you can get someone to open up to you and discuss themselves, and what they need, the better! This helps funnel your prospect down through the yes chain. If you actually listen to their needs and wants, it yields to a higher closing rate more often than not. Remember, this isn't always so! People do funny things when feeling pressure—be aware, be nice, and be the person you would want to buy from! HELP THEM, DON'T SCREW THEM!

Okay, so we touched base on some objections, but how do you really know where to go once you get an objection? It's simple, if you show your care, you've demonstrated knowledge of your company, product or service, objections will often result into the same set, and once you're proficient at pitching, many will just go away due to the fact that you answered them before they arose.

So, what else do we say about objections? These are the problems that many salespeople have difficulty with. I have no magic solution to tell you how to deal with these. Each industry is different; each industry has different main objections. You need to study, seek guidance from those who are top performers, your managers, etc. STUDY, LEARN, APPLY, AND REPEAT!

Chapter Eleven

Referrals?

What is that?

How does a good salesperson move up the ladder to greatness? It's simple: referrals! Referrals are by far the best lead a salesperson can get. Just look at the top performers in your industry and ask those people how they do it. Many, if not all, will tell you they sell from referrals.

What is a referral? A referral is someone who believes in you and your product or service enough to tell others. If you ask for referrals, you up your chance of getting referrals from zero to 50%. This helps to increase your overall profit margin and paycheck!

How can we get those? Many ways!

One of the easiest and most simplified ways is to just ask your current customers to give them to you. Guess what, that sounds way easier said than done. Most of your customers are NOT just going to give you referrals right away.

Okay, so how do we do that? Well for one, if you followed the basics of this book, it's simple: be genuine! Meaning, do what you said you were going to do, when, and what you promised you would do. In today's social media age, people are more likely to refer to others they trust who took great care of them. Be that person! Take great care of all of your customers and do it because you want to. Your customers will see and feel the care and will be more likely to tell others about you.

Most people who believe in you and/or buy from you, want to refer you, but don't always do so. In today's age with social media, people are more important as a source of generating new business than regular marketing. Referrals have become a huge medium for new sales! Times have changed from where to spend marketing dollars to get new customers to call, to who is talking about your company in order to refer you. Make yourself stand out, be the person people choose to refer via social media. In order to do that, you need to care about your customer and make them feel that you and your company are the best choice. Also, you must be there when they need you!

For example, a job you just sold is going on a day you scheduled it—be there for it, make sure what you promised is in line with what your company offers, and is done correctly, then talk to the neighbors, or other tenants if commercial or multi-family. Then, follow up to make sure they're happy, or if they need additional service, schedule it for them. Take care of your customers so they in turn take care of you!

During your initial presentation you should bring up referrals and let them know you want them, but you don't have to ask for them right then and there. During follow-up, see if all is well, and then ask for them either on social media or right then.

This chapter is short, but one of the most important! At each presentation you do, you should discuss referrals and explain how they help others as well as you! It has to be a win-win for both. Many companies offer incentives for referrals, but you should seek these out for your own wellbeing.

I witnessed my Dad when we were on a sales call get 26 referrals off one lead, just because he asked who else do you know that could benefit from our service. Our customer handed him her rolodex full of names! All he did was ask, and so should you. The reason being, if you don't ever ask, the answer to that question is always NO!

Now, depending on the industry you're in, the time to ask for those referrals differs. Sometimes you may not only have to deliver on that first round of service, but it may take a few services to cultivate the relationship to the point that, that customer is ready to speak kindly of you to others.

The keys to referrals are this: If you don't ask, the answer is NO! The other key is this: make sure your current customer is well taken care of, and they're more likely to refer you and your company to others!

Yes, you can get referrals on the first visit or pitch. However, most of the time people want to see if you deliver what you say you will before they're willing to reciprocate. Which means you need to follow up and make sure your customers receive what you promised!

Chapter Twelve

Paradigm

Paradigm? What is this? Why is this the last chapter? Is it just because I wanted to end it here, or is it because I saved the best for last?

Here is the actual definition of paradigm from Webster's: a philosophical and theoretical framework of a scientific school or discipline within which theories, laws, and generalizations and the experiments performed in support of them are formulated; *broadly*: a philosophical or theoretical framework of any kind

So based on the above what do we say about this? Here are my thoughts. Paradigm is nothing more than reality. Well, what is reality? Reality is nothing more than the way a person perceives the world in their mind and opinion. Reality is different for everyone. We all see the world differently, and we need to understand and respect this. Our job as sales representatives is to bridge the gaps, identify needs and wants, and figure out how we can help our customers within their paradigm. Meaning how do they perceive you and what you can do for them. Customer perception can also equal do they buy from us and are they willing to refer us to others. Your job, as their representative, is to become the contact they tell everyone else about.

What does that mean according to sales? It's simple, how many times have you walked out of a presentation, didn't get the sale, and sat there going "Ohhhh they just didn't see the need?" (or some other form of self-allowance to reassure yourself that it was justifiable that you didn't close the sale?)

More often than not, salespeople focus on what they want or need, even when they're trying their hardest to focus on their customer! We're humans; our sales practice needs to focus on the needs and wants of our customers and actually listen to their needs and wants in order to discover do I even have something they need or want. Avoid just trying to sell them something! I've made many sales from referrals (listed above) because I told the truth, whereas others may have said what they wanted to hear, in order to get a quick commission.

Can you make a ton of money by just doing this and that to get a sale? Sure you can! Can you honestly look at yourself in the mirror? Not many can! I prefer sleeping well at night as well as my customers saying, "Call so-and-so, they'll take great care of you!"

Basically, to be truly great in sales, you must separate yourself from yourself, understand your customers' wants and needs, or paradigm, and then figure out how to help them in a way that promotes happiness and thankfulness on their part, while taking care of your customer!

My final take: if you really want to increase your sales, start understanding your prospects' paradigm! The reason why: paradigm has a completely different meaning to all of us, and if you want to maximize your ability then you need to understand others and what they like, don't like, want, need, and don't need!

Yes, this is a short and sweet chapter, but a very important one nonetheless!

Happy Trails and God Speed!

Chapter Thirteen

Final Acknowledgements

Many, many nights were spent with me writing and editing this book while my kids were sleeping.

I had my companies to run during the day as well as triplets to help take care of, and day to day household chores to tend to while working on this book. This has taken numerous years to finally finish.

I was encouraged by numerous people that I trained in sales to write a book, and I finally decided to do so. This book was created solely from my knowledge, experience, and learning from other sales trainers throughout the years.

I studied sales from numerous other people; while writing this book, I wanted to focus on what I learned and what I could teach and therefore wrote my knowledge and experience as it relates to this field, while writing this book! I chose to be as authentic as I could, for my sake and yours, even though there's only so much we can learn and teach others in regard to sales.

I've spent countless hours and numerous really late nights trying to put this book together. I have my own companies to run during regular hours, triplets to take care of, homework, and sports outside normal business hours, so **NO** writing self-help books is **NOT** my normal thing! I seriously want this book to help others!

To my friends: Thank you for your support and continued encouragement! Writing this book was a major undertaking.

The thing about sales is, it's always evolving, and you must constantly keep learning and practicing! Learn, practice, learn!

Chapter Fourteen

About the Author

Let me introduce myself. Hi, it's me Chris. I've spent over 25 years in sales, sales management, and business ownership that required sales. Let me first explain why I wrote this book. I originally started writing this book for my own benefit. I wasn't looking for anyone else to read my words until a few of my sales friends found out that I was putting my own words down. Some of them told me that I should write a book on sales. I decided to do that, and now here I am delivering my knowledge, skills, and studies to all of you, and I hope you benefit from it!

Over the course of my sales career, one of the most major factors that helped me be successful in sales was effective communication. Having an interest in other people, and actually listening to what they want, need, and desire, made me jump far ahead of others. When we perform sales, it's NOT about us and what we want! It's completely about those we go to see and pitch what we have to offer. We must match wants, needs, and desires, with what we're selling.

I've spent almost 3 decades in sales and sales management. Before that, I spent 8 years in the special warfare realm of the Air Force as a TACP. That career field helped me build on a foundation already laid out by my Dad who was a professional salesperson of over 25 years.

I've spent almost 18 years writing this book. Yes, it has taken me quite a while. Honestly, I never actually planned on publishing my book, until now. I worked on this book off and on for many years, and it used to help me get back on track when I felt off course from closing sales from time to time. Yeah, the best of the best can veer off track occasionally. A good friend of mine convinced me to publish this book, and for whoever reads it, may you achieve great success and take care of others at the same time!

My past credentials:

- Top sales/sales manager performance
- BS in Aviation Management, graduated Magna Cum Laude
- Real Estate License, used for commercial real estate
- Health and Life Insurance License
- Private Pilot License
- Structural Pest Control License in WDO and HPC
- Former TACP with JTAC qualifications in US Air Force
- IFOR Peacekeeper 1996 in Sarajevo, Bosnia
- Top performing sales representative and sales manager

www.ingramcontent.com/pod-product-compliance
Lightning Source LLC
Chambersburg PA
CBHW020608030426
42337CB00013B/1272